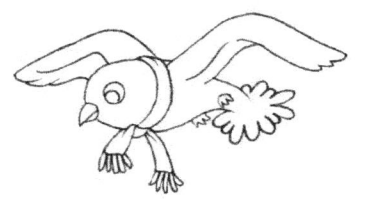

Animals and Peace

a book designed for coloring

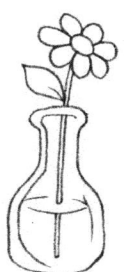

Queenie Wong

ISBN-13: 978-1533206107
ISBN-10: 1533206104
First published in United States in 2016
Illustrations by Queenie Wong
Wonger0050@yahoo.com.hk

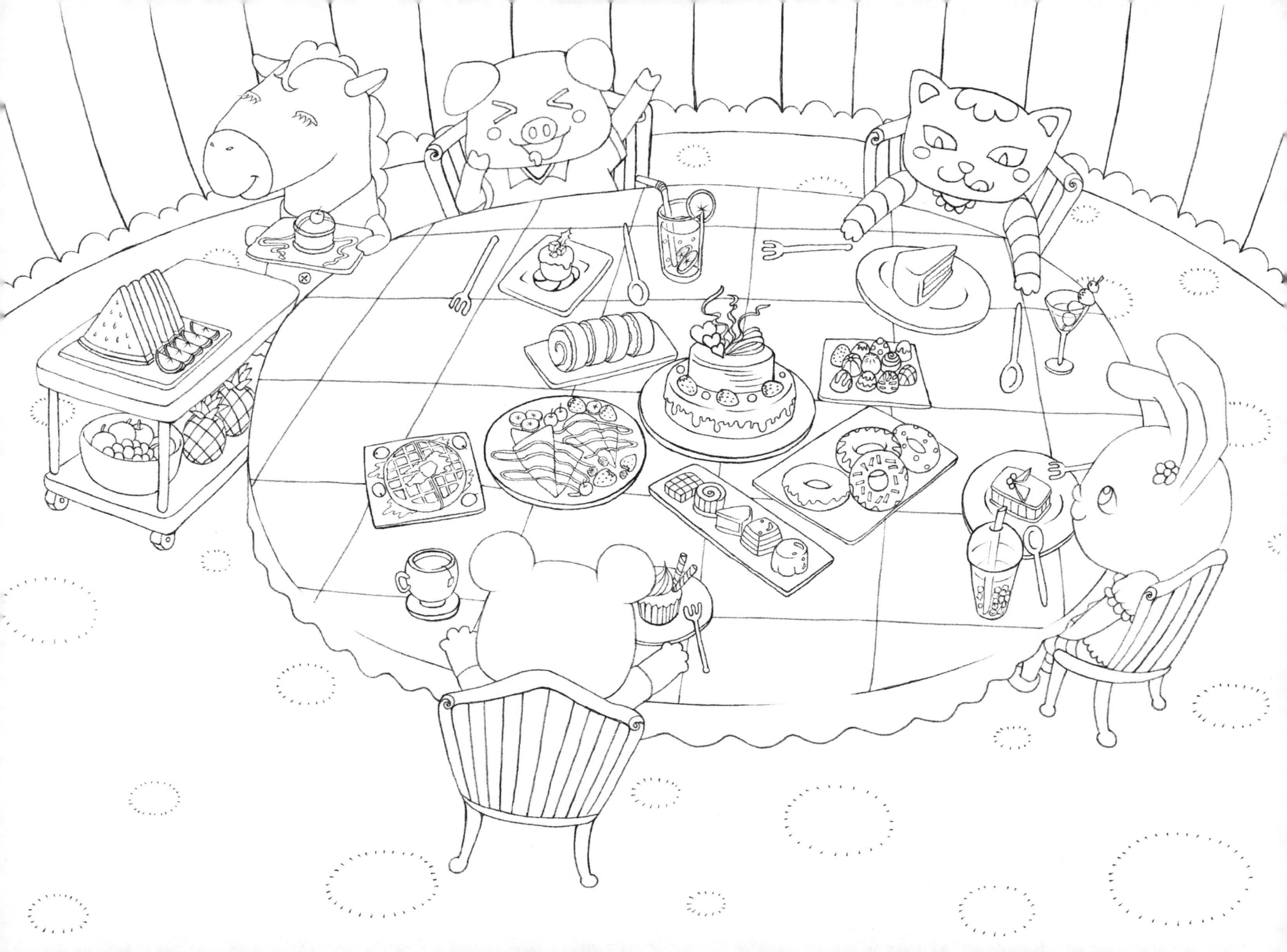

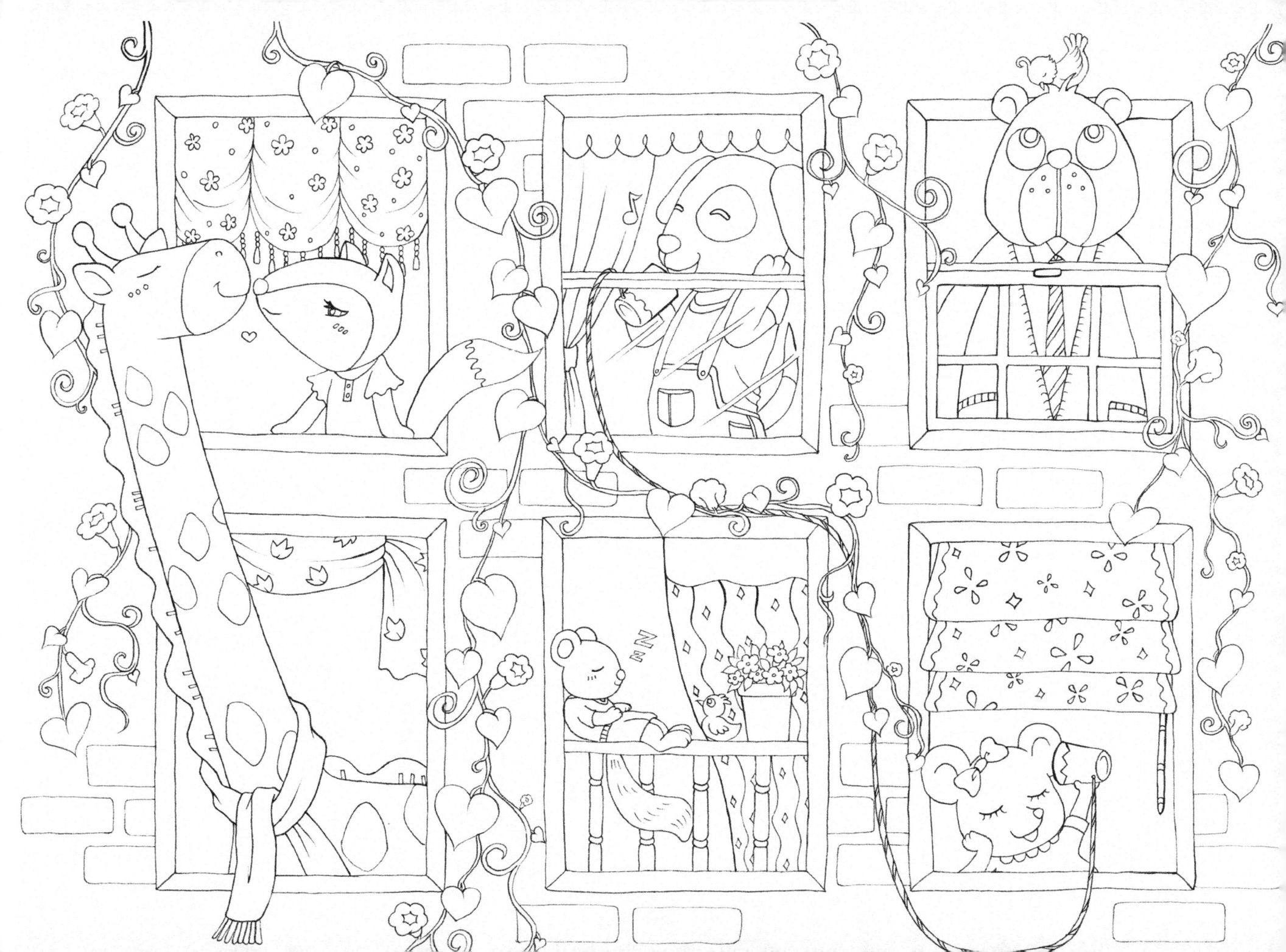

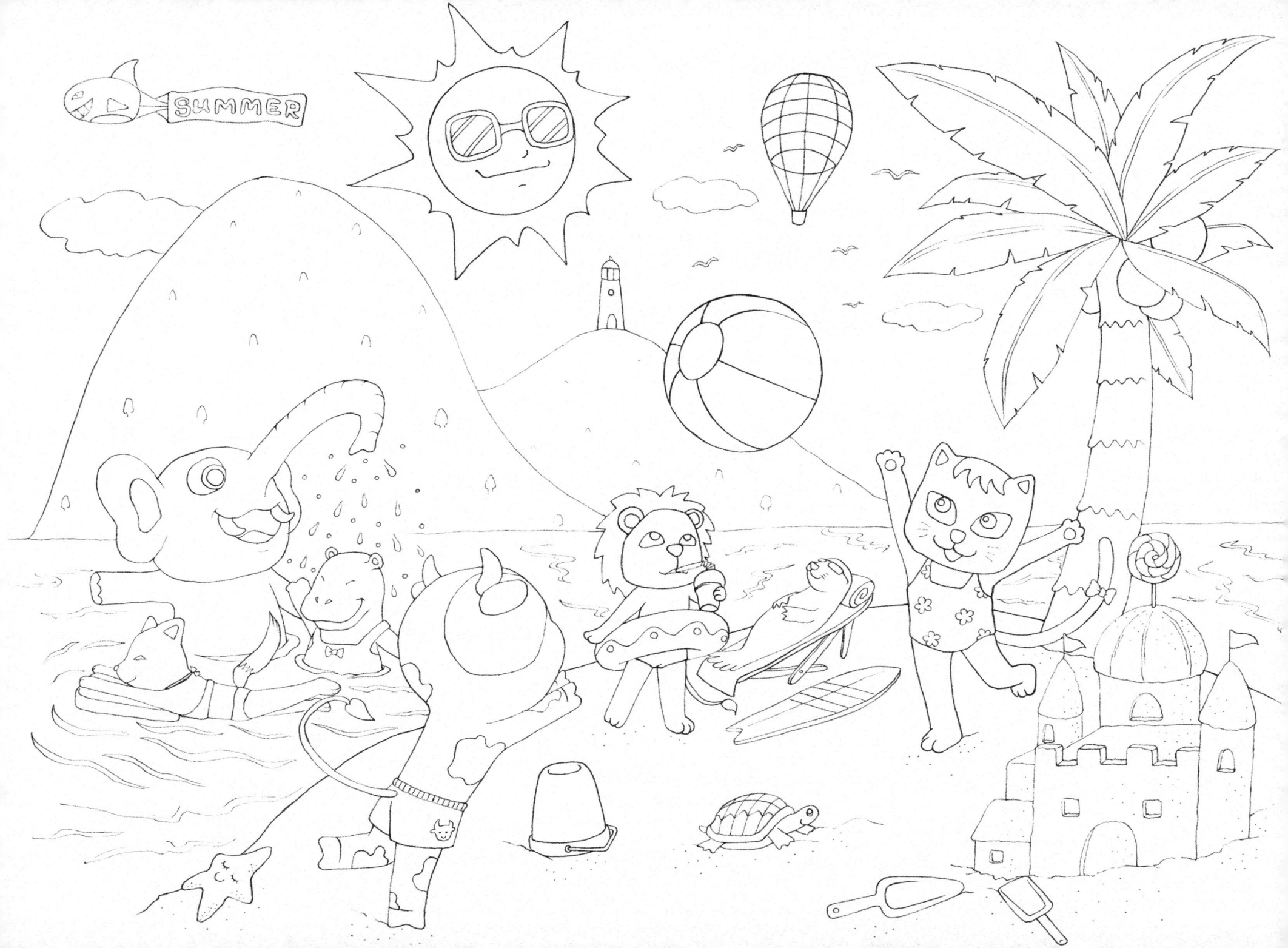

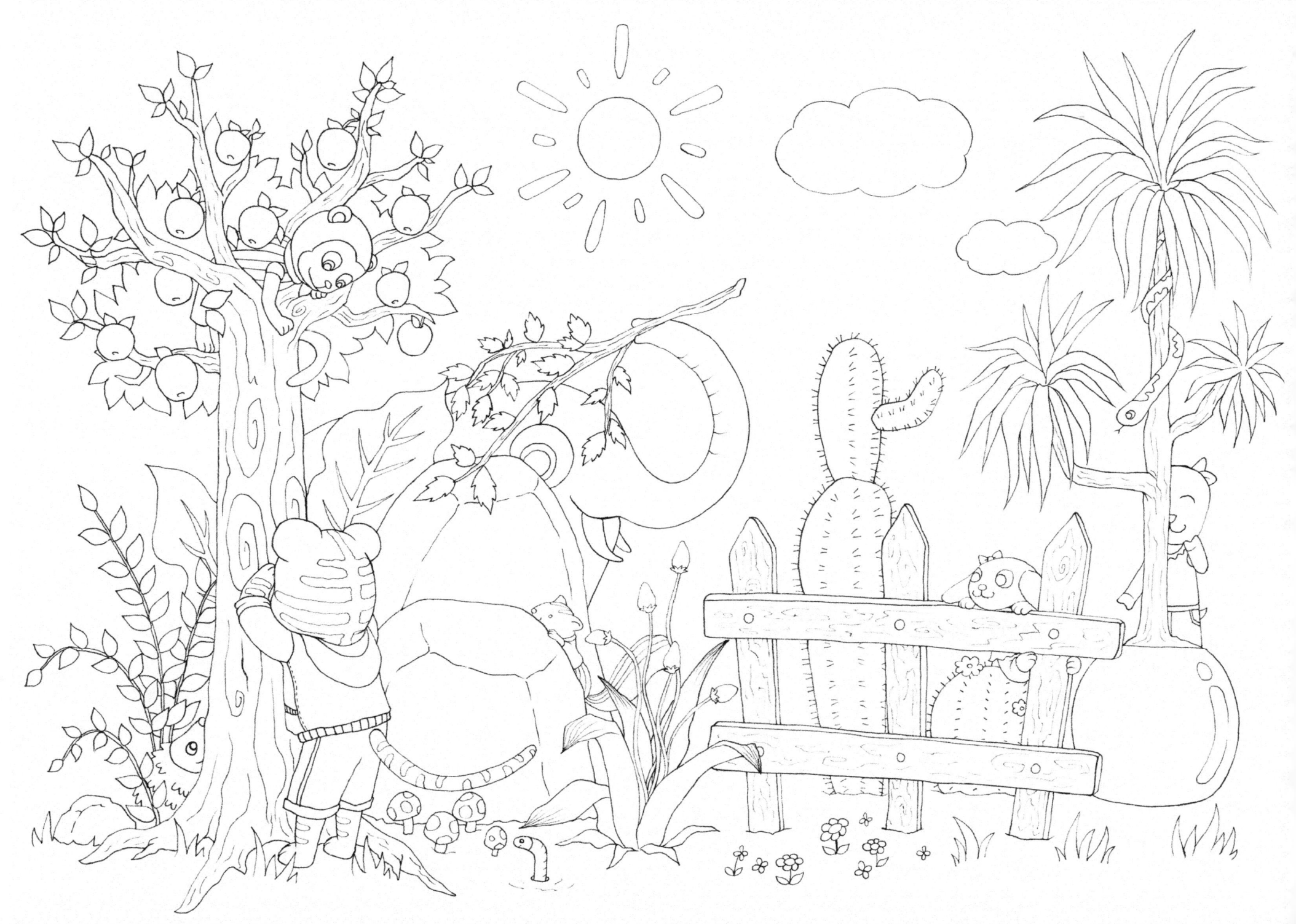

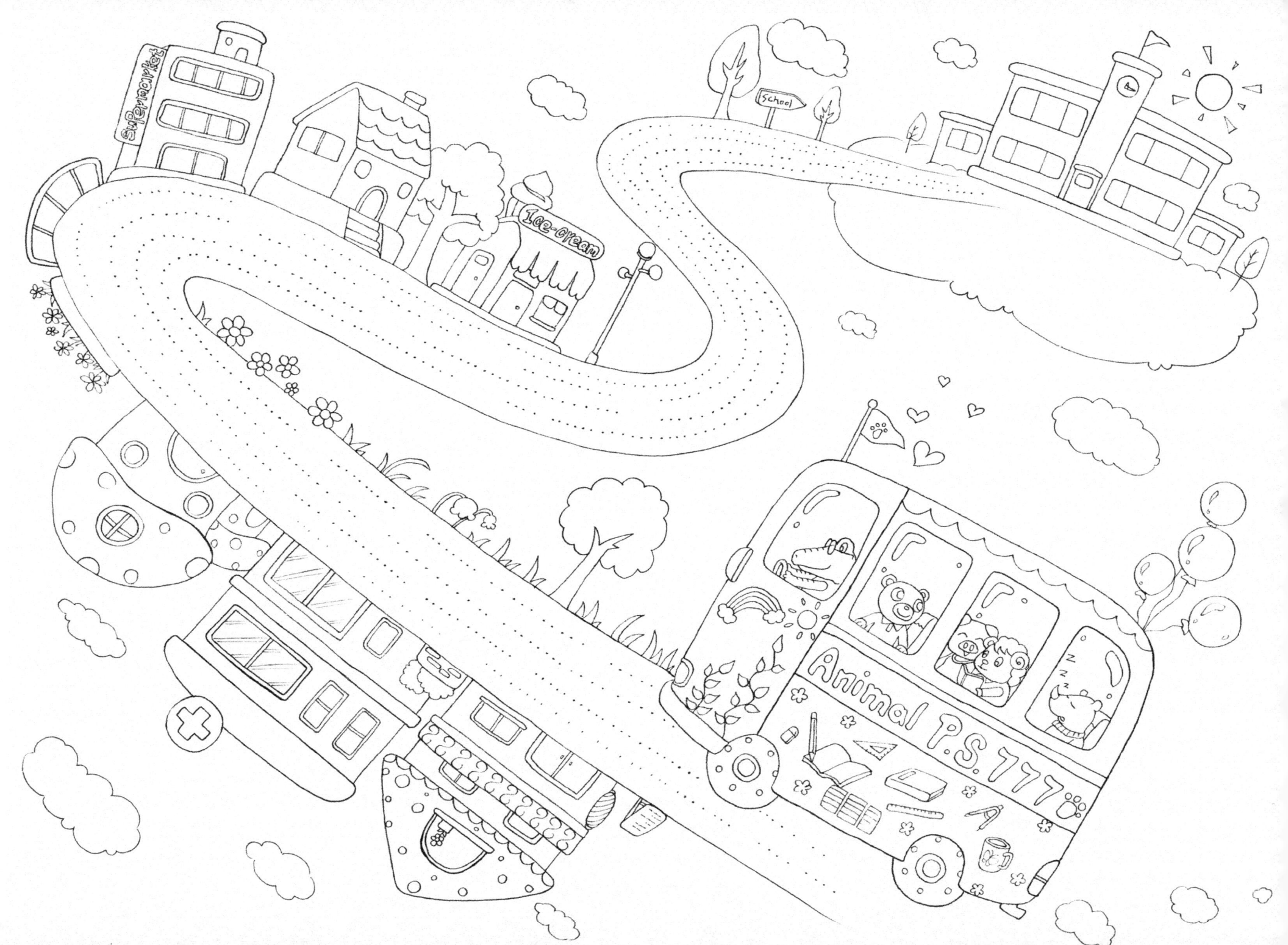

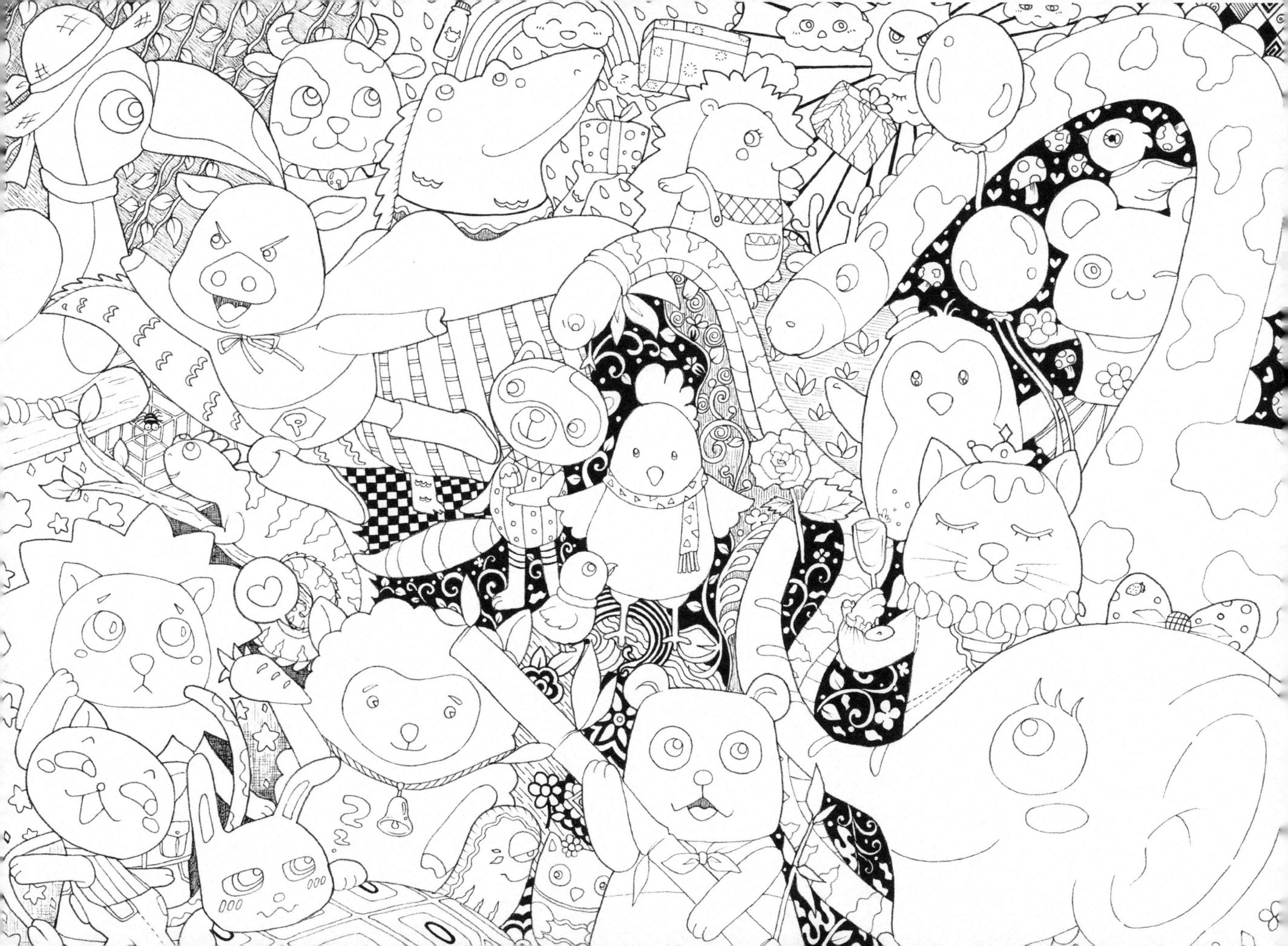

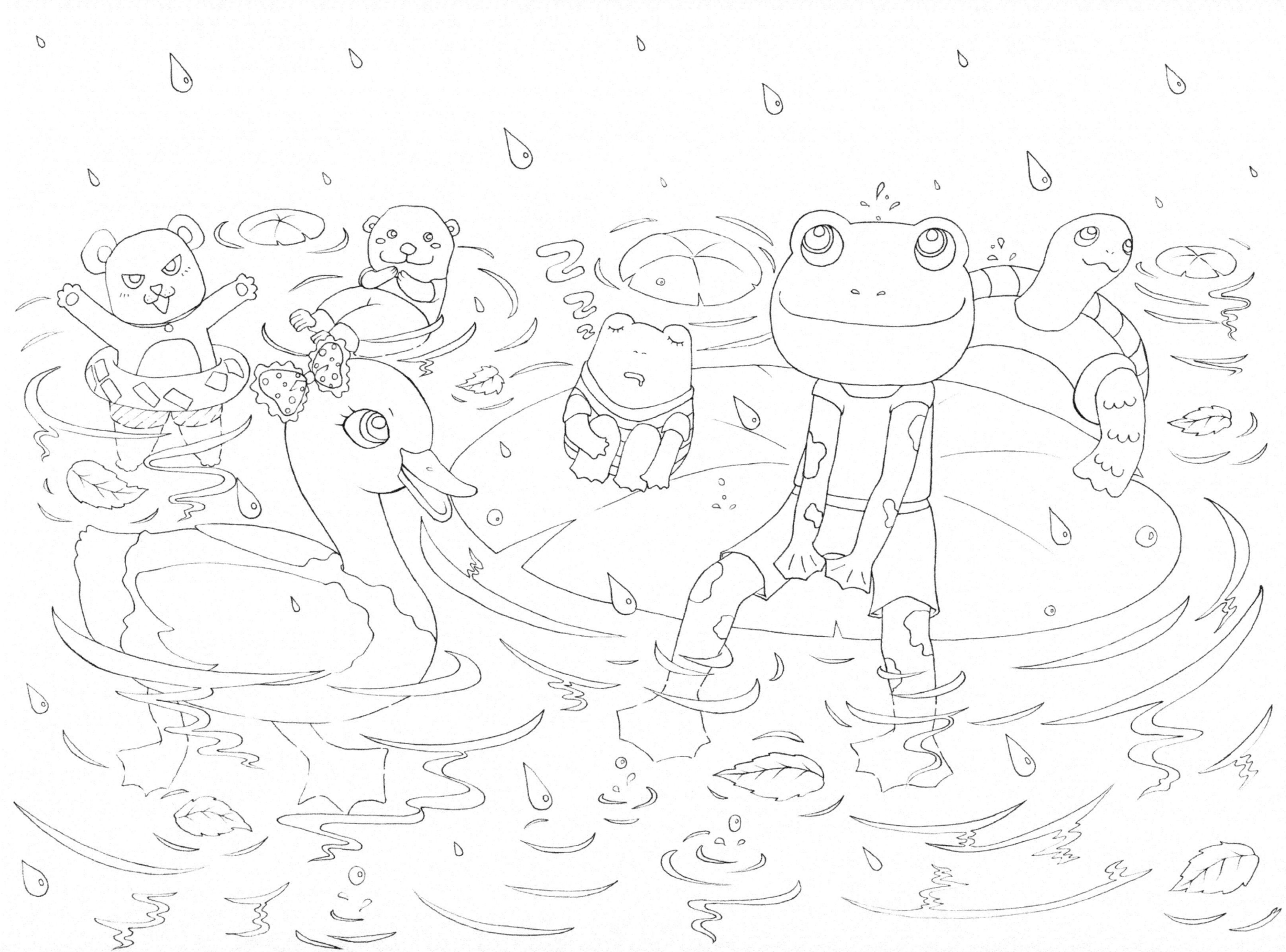

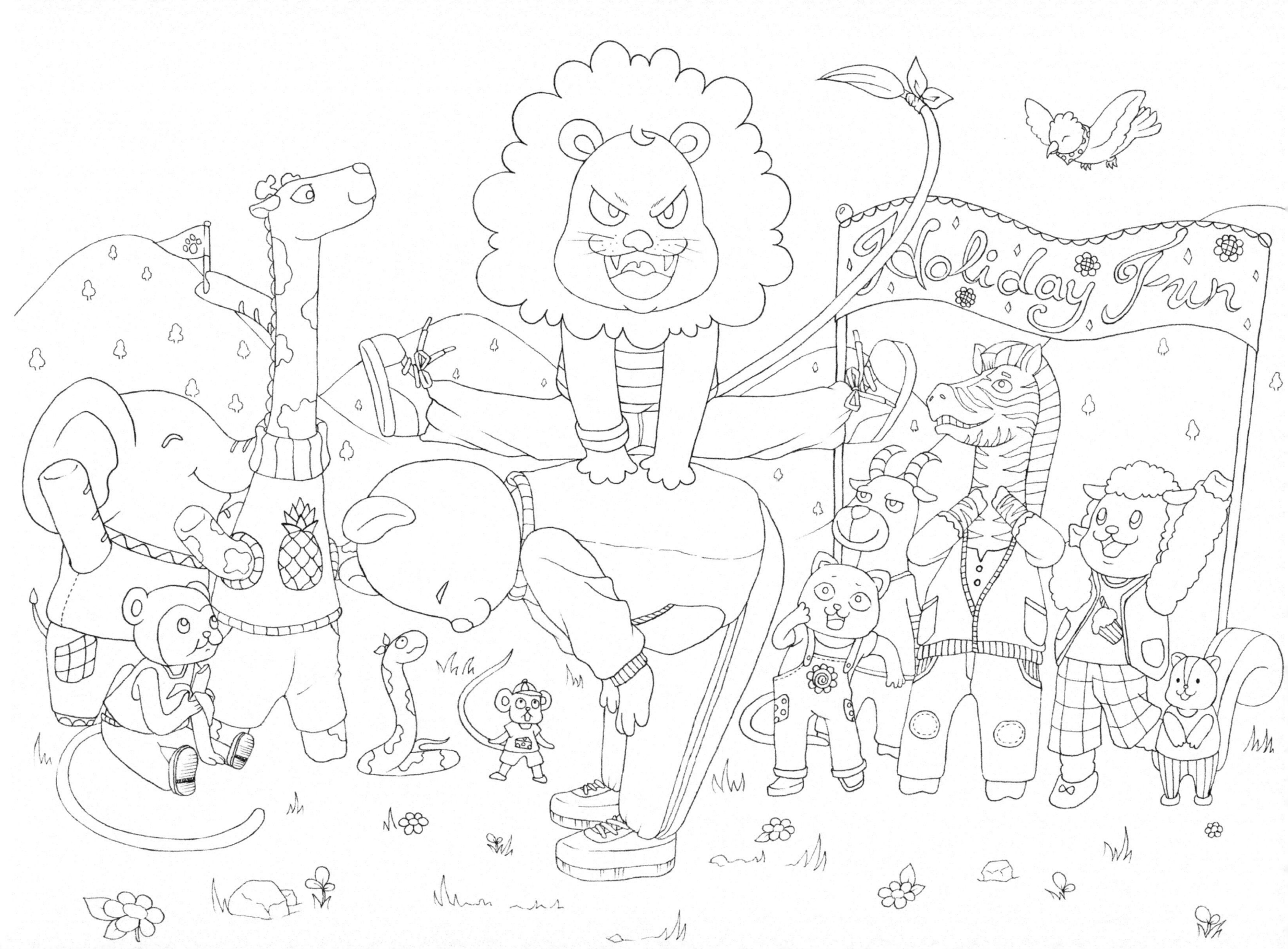

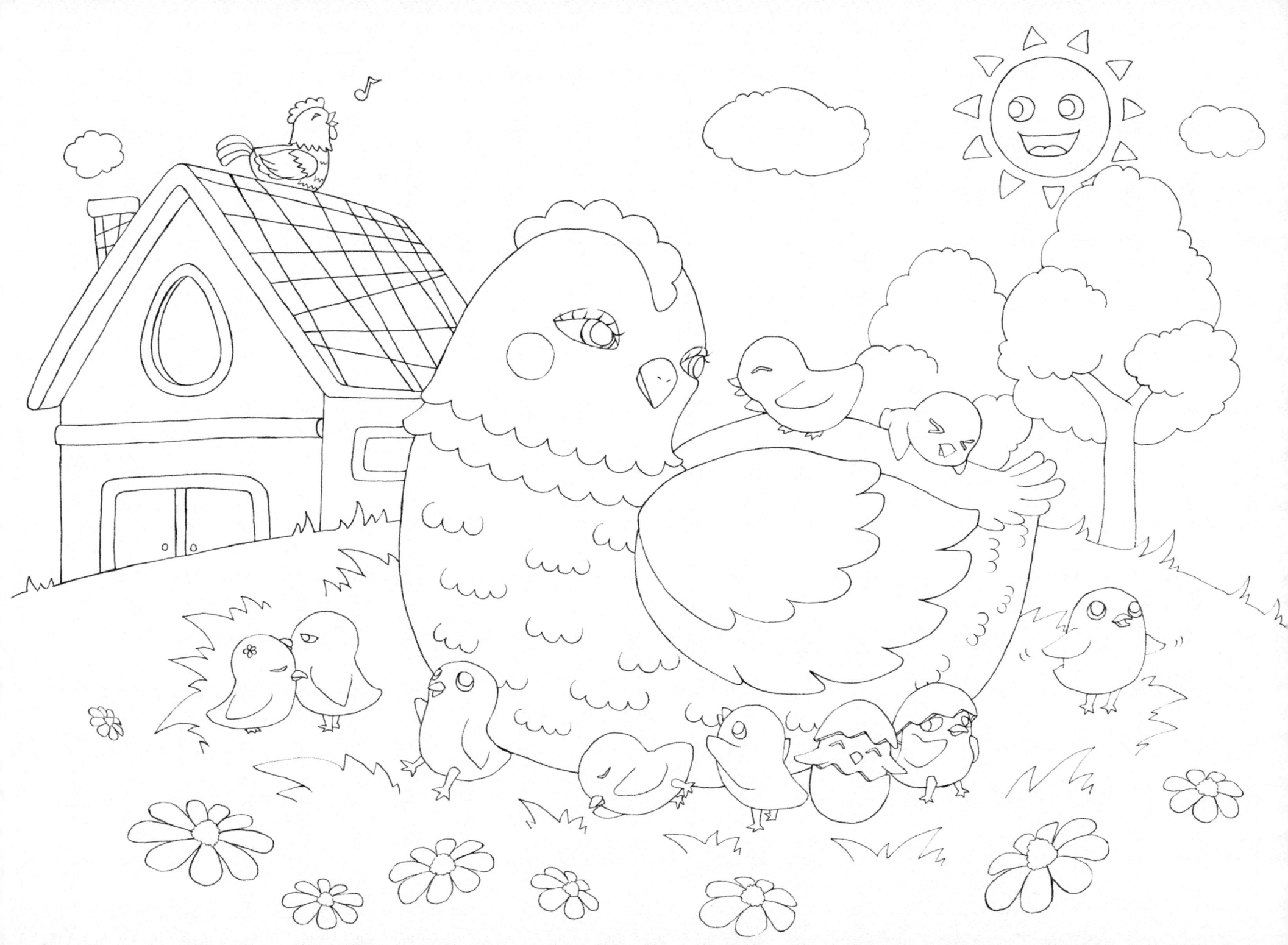

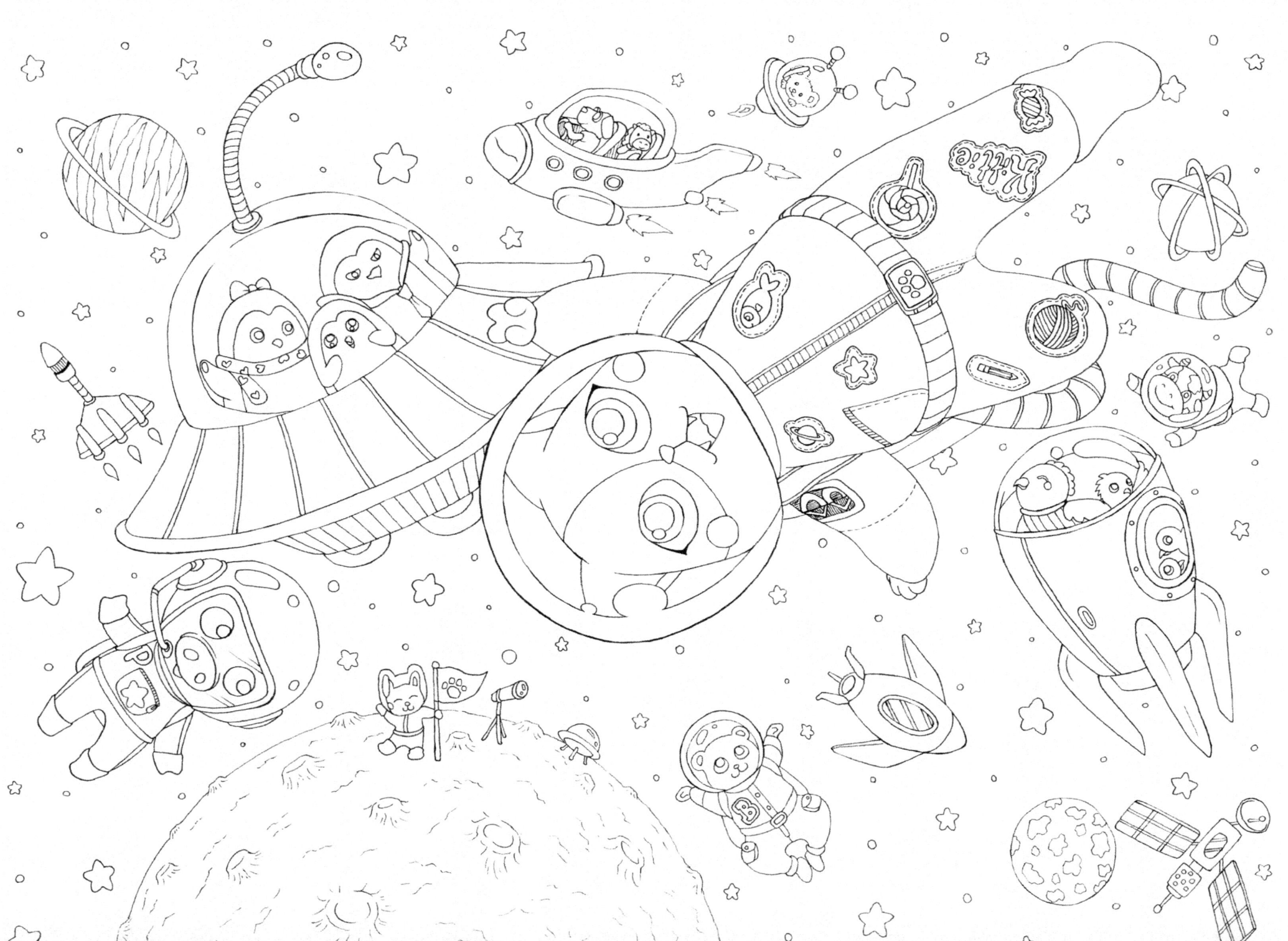

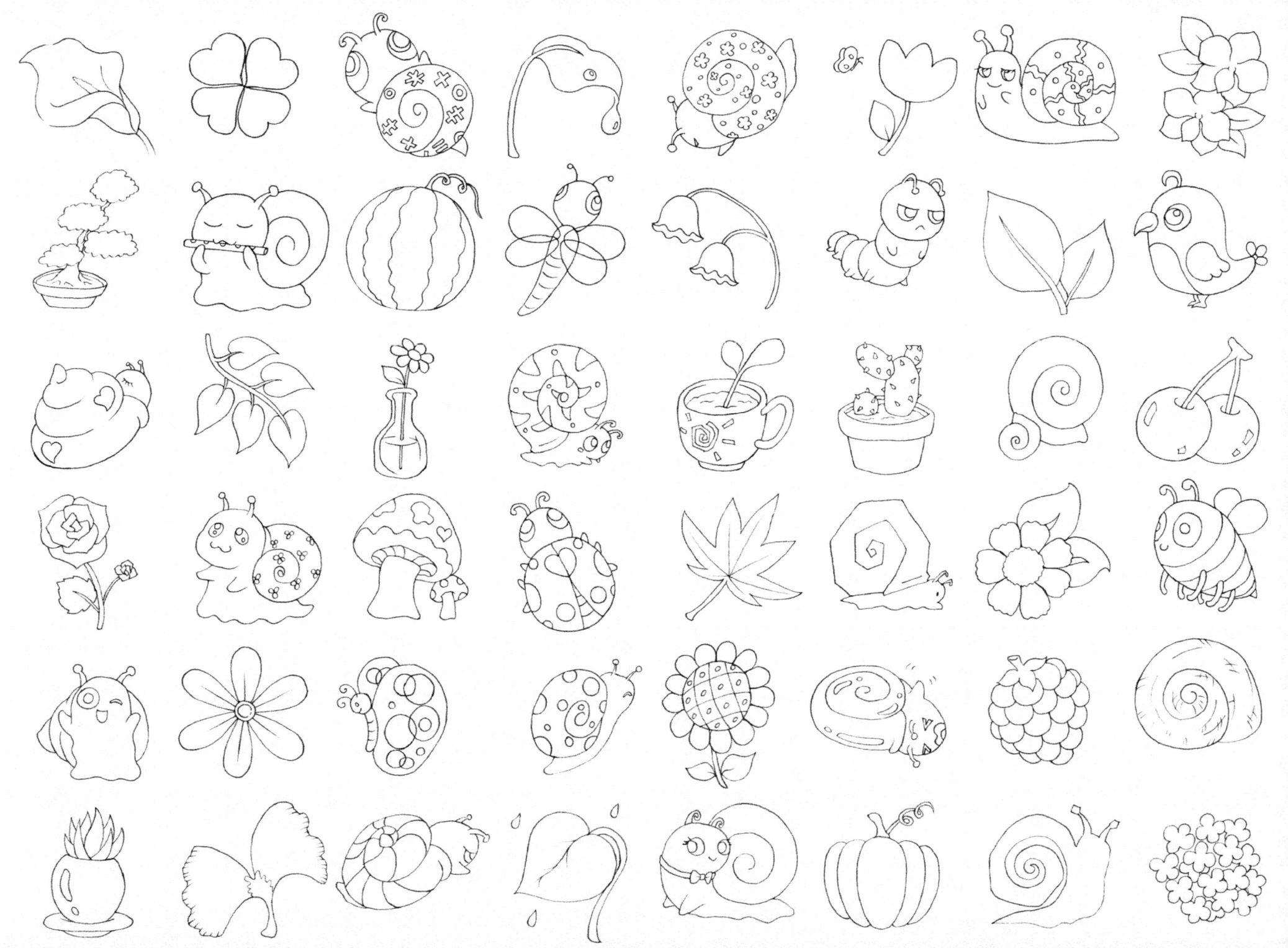

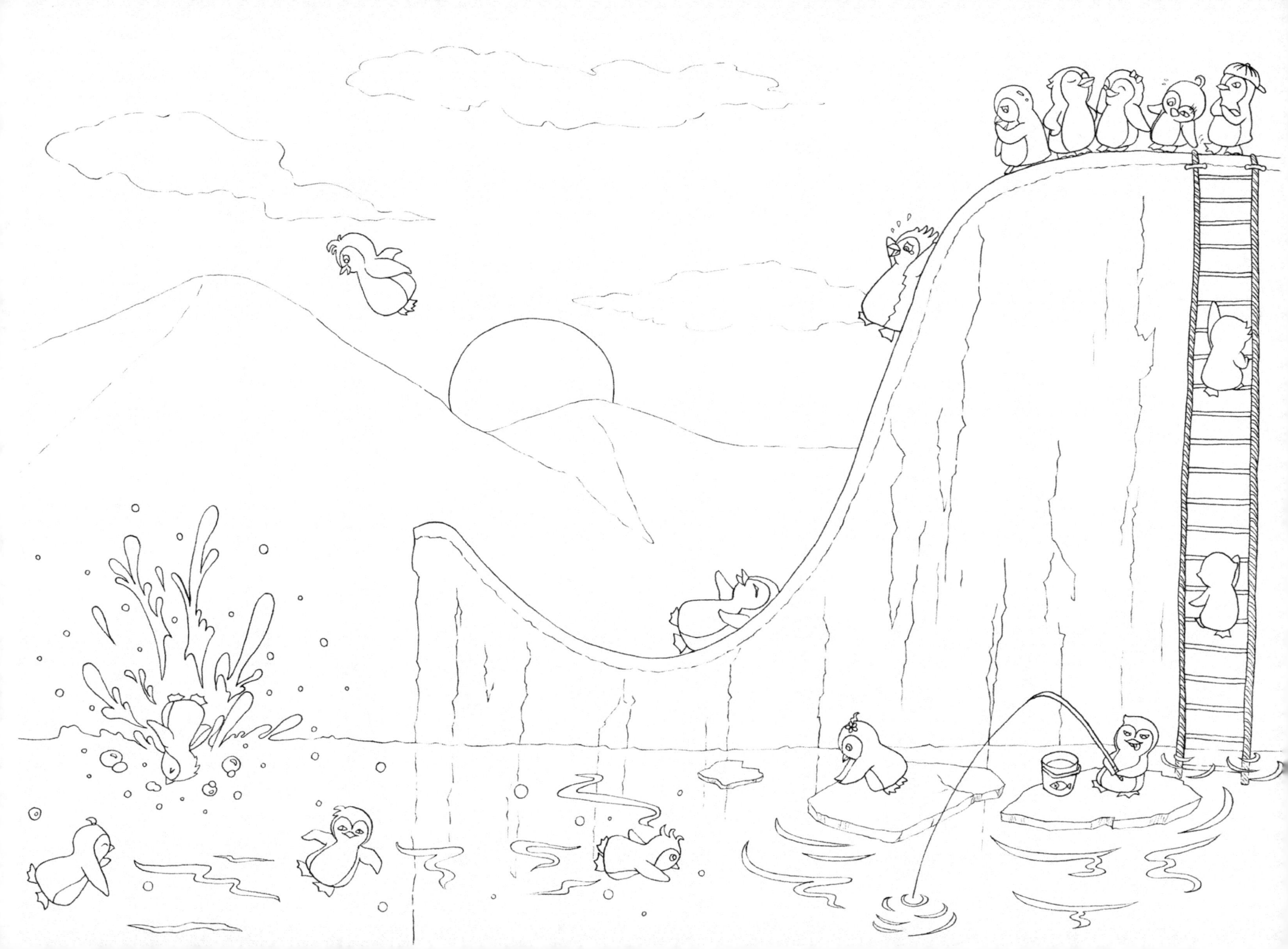

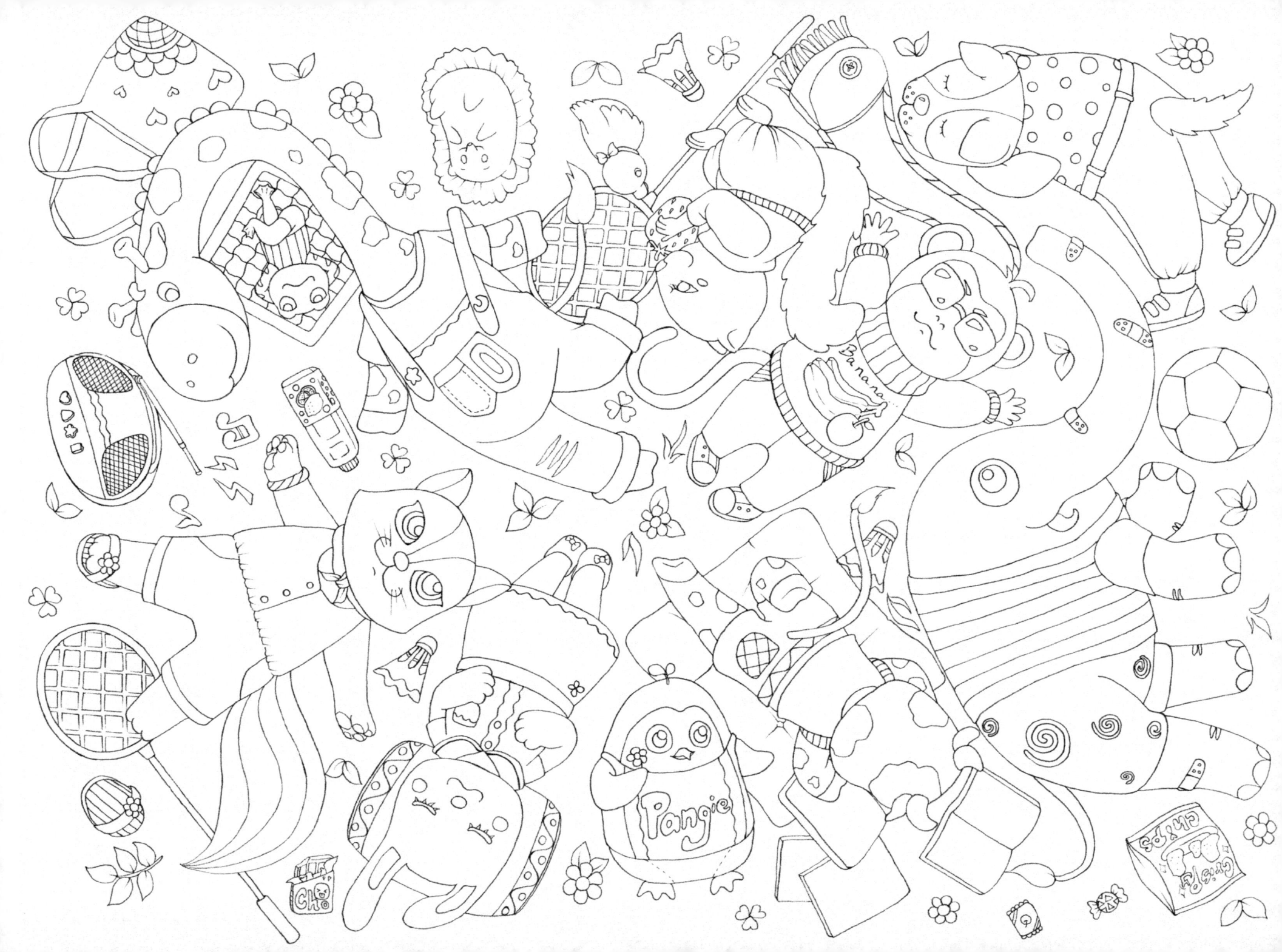

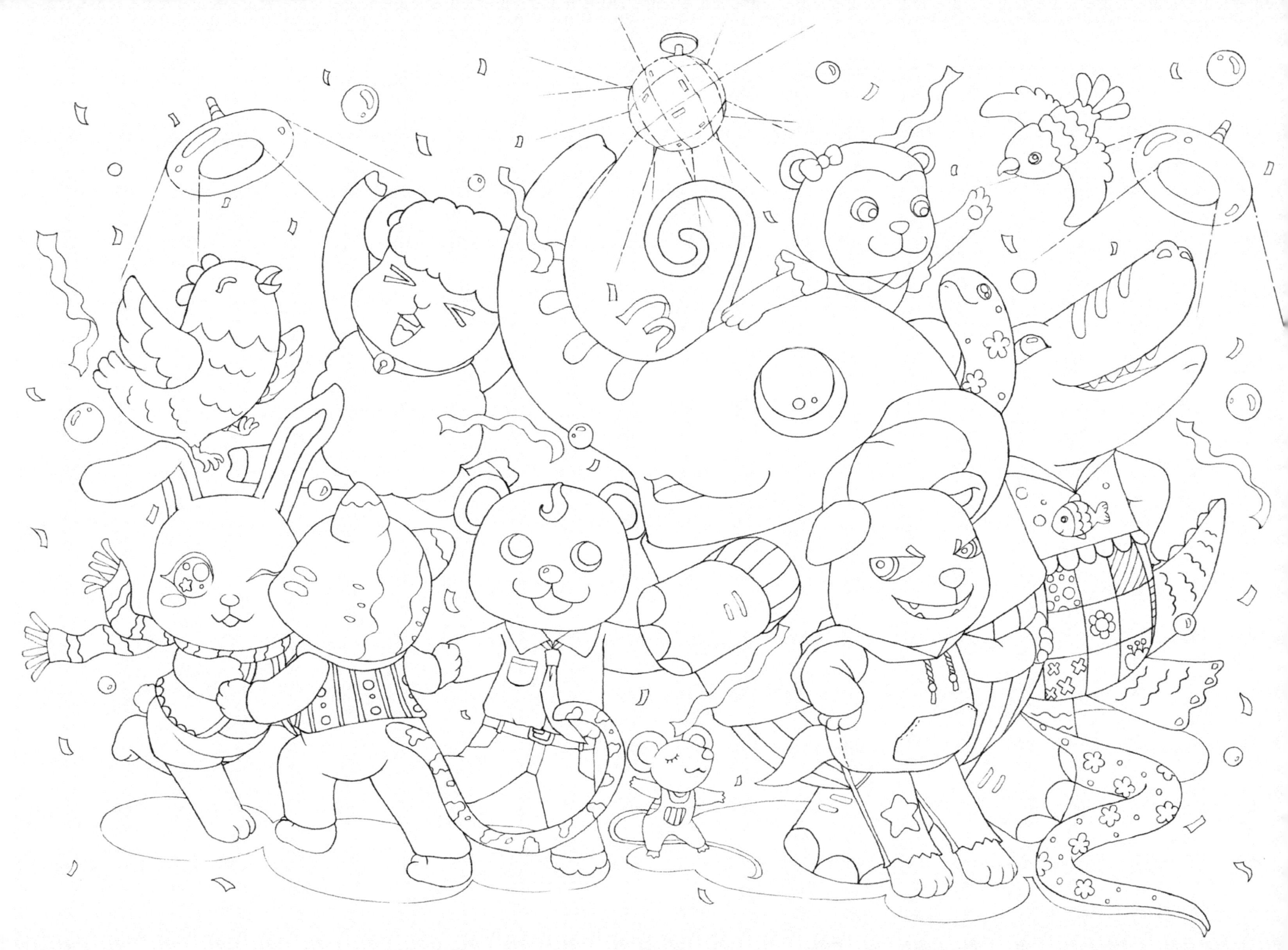

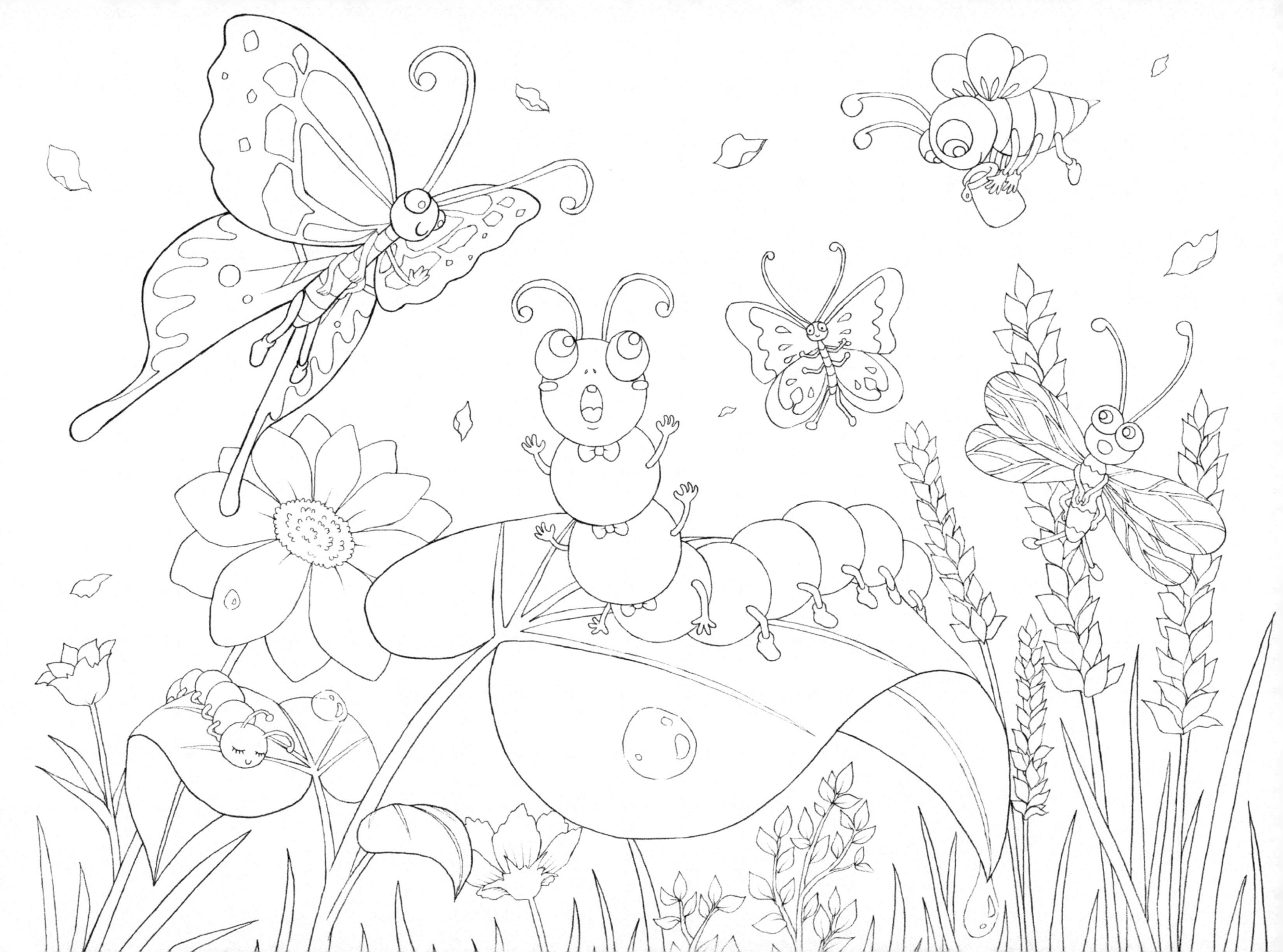

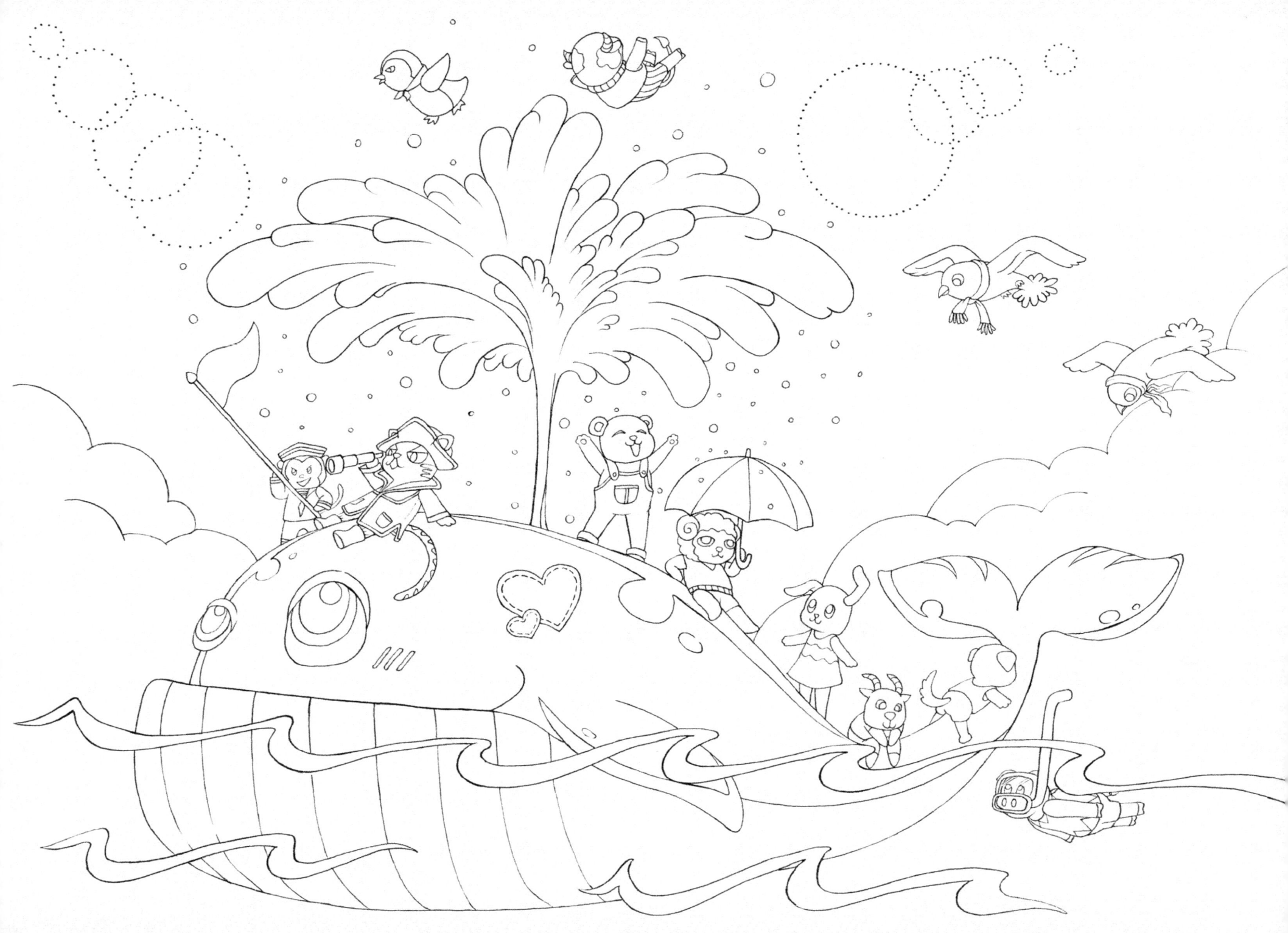

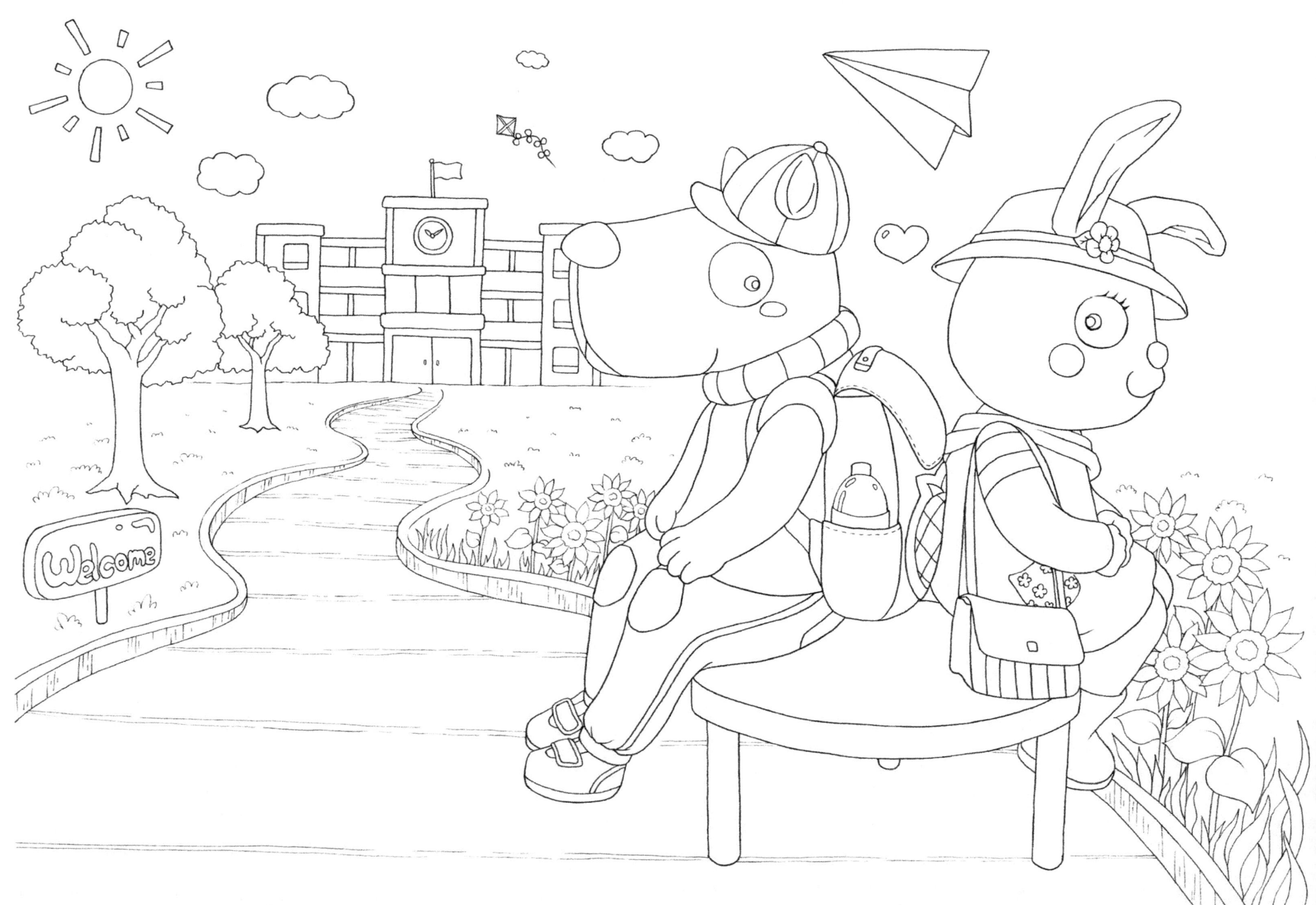

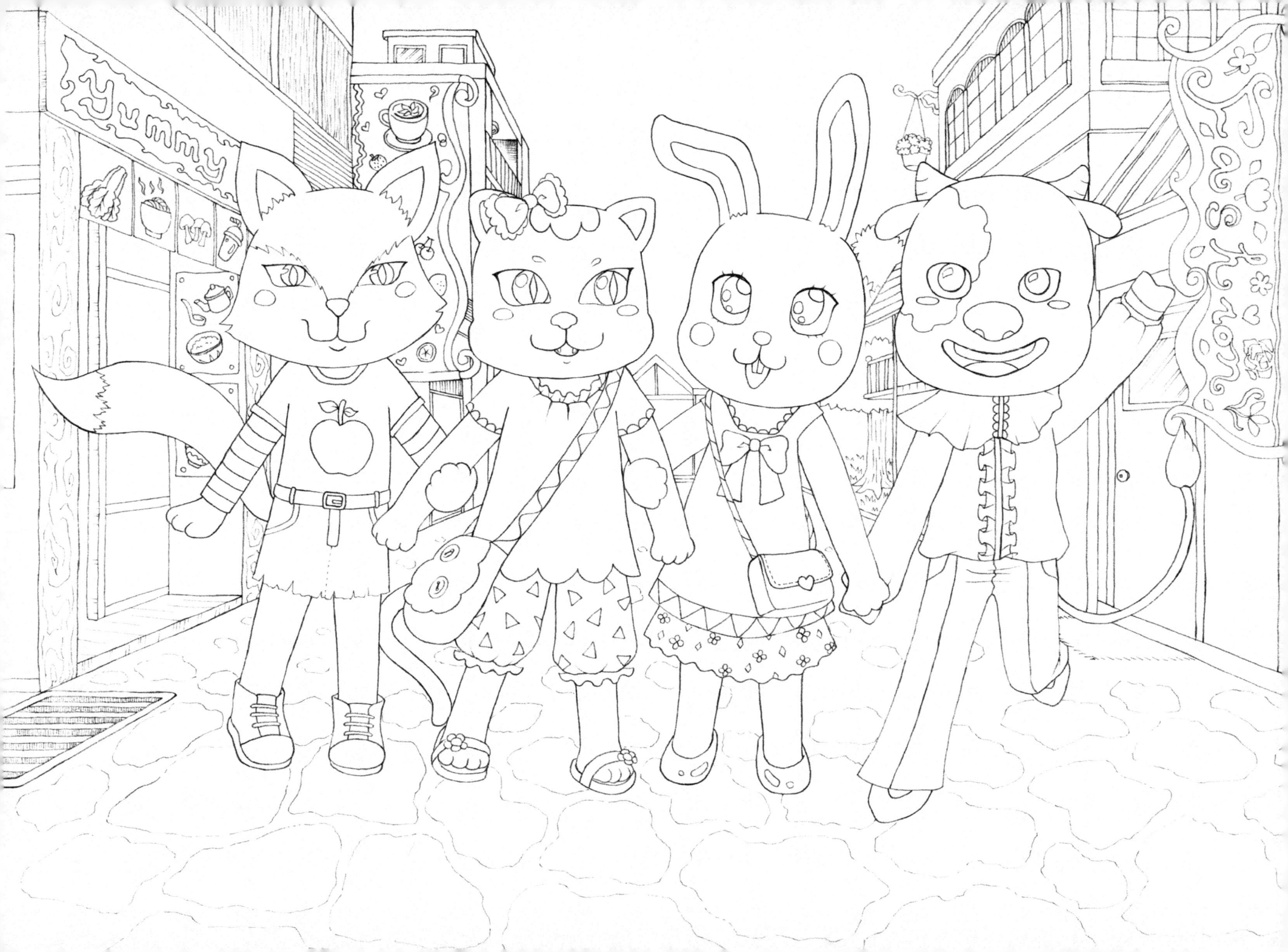

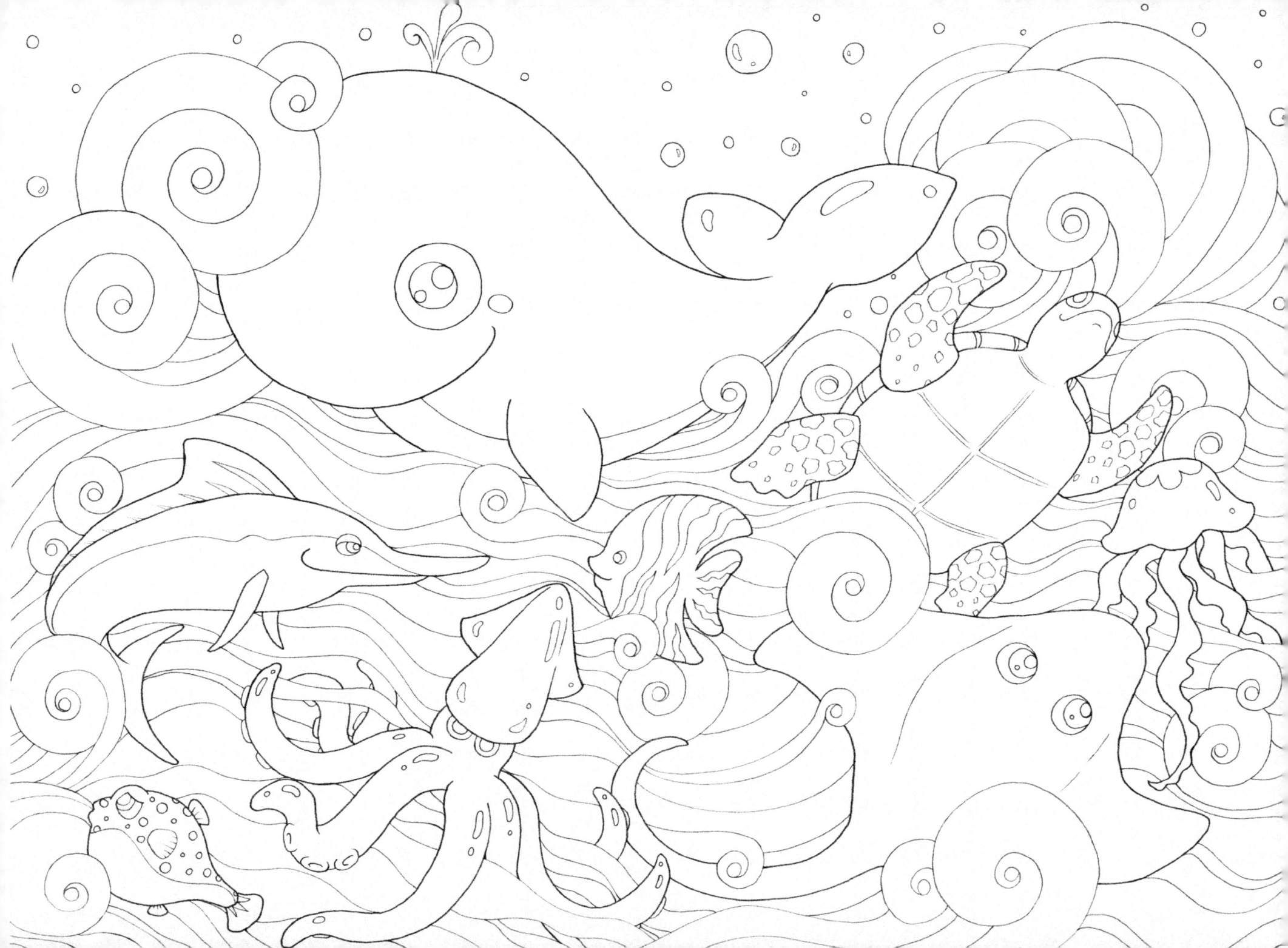

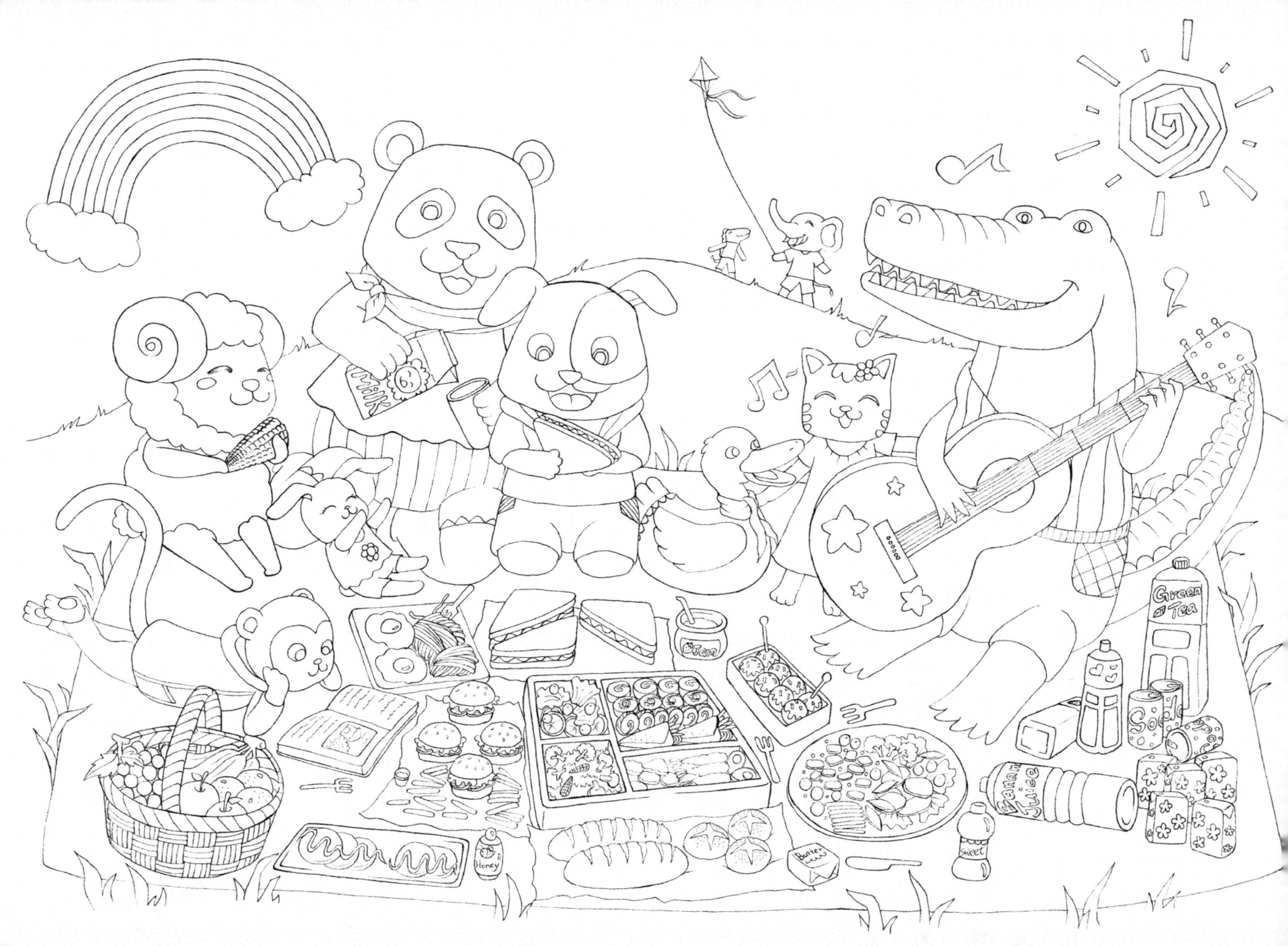

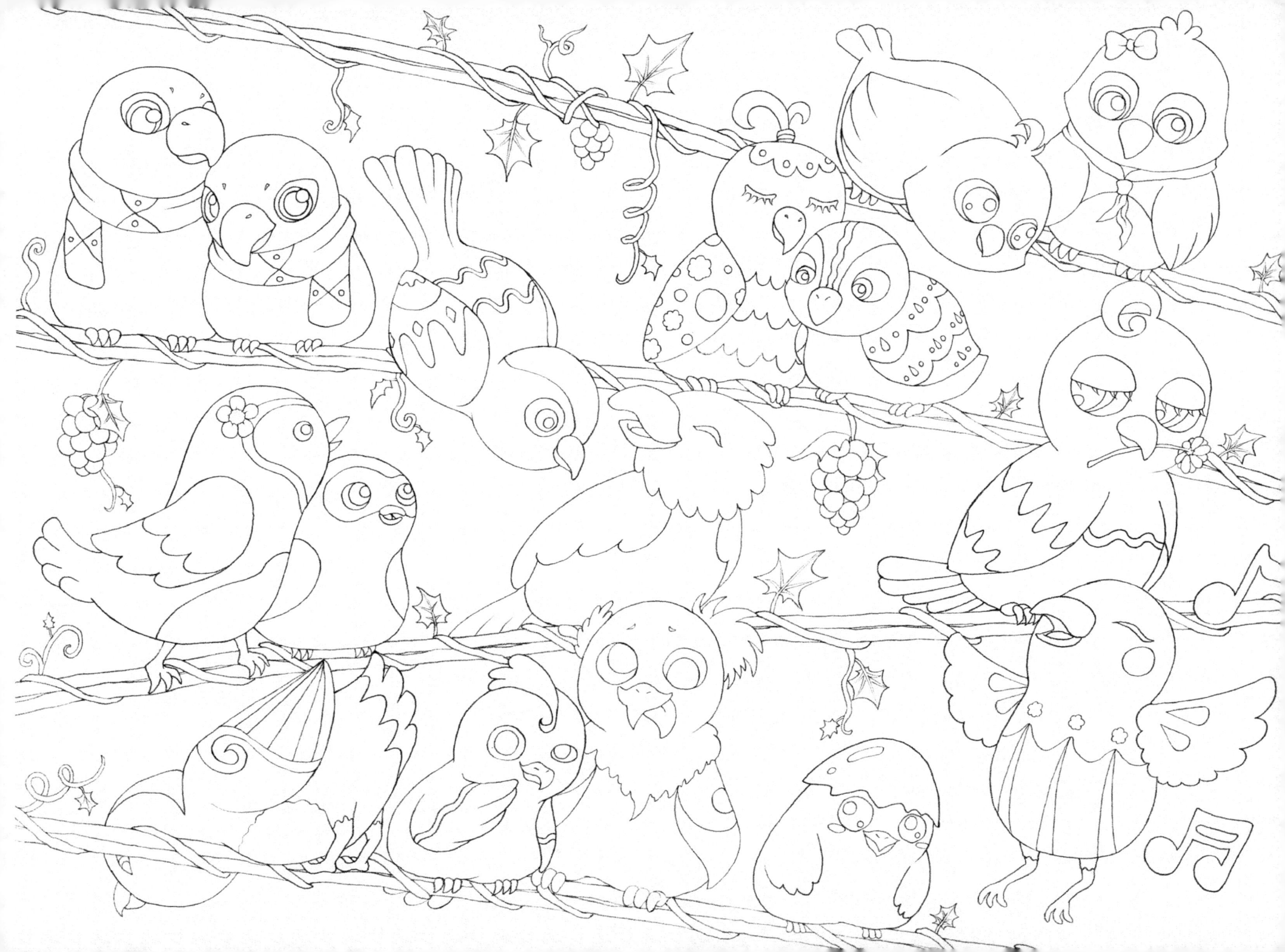

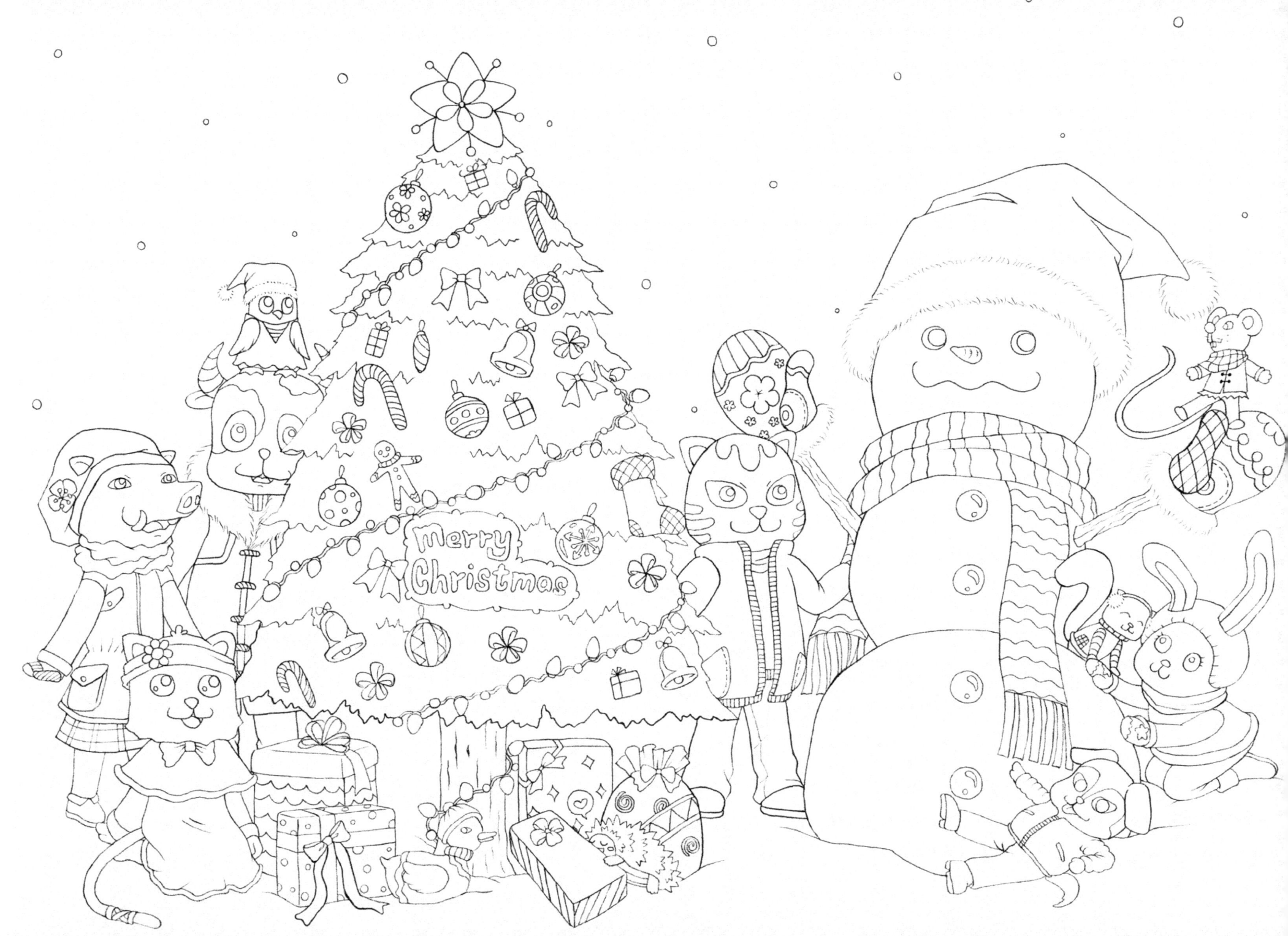

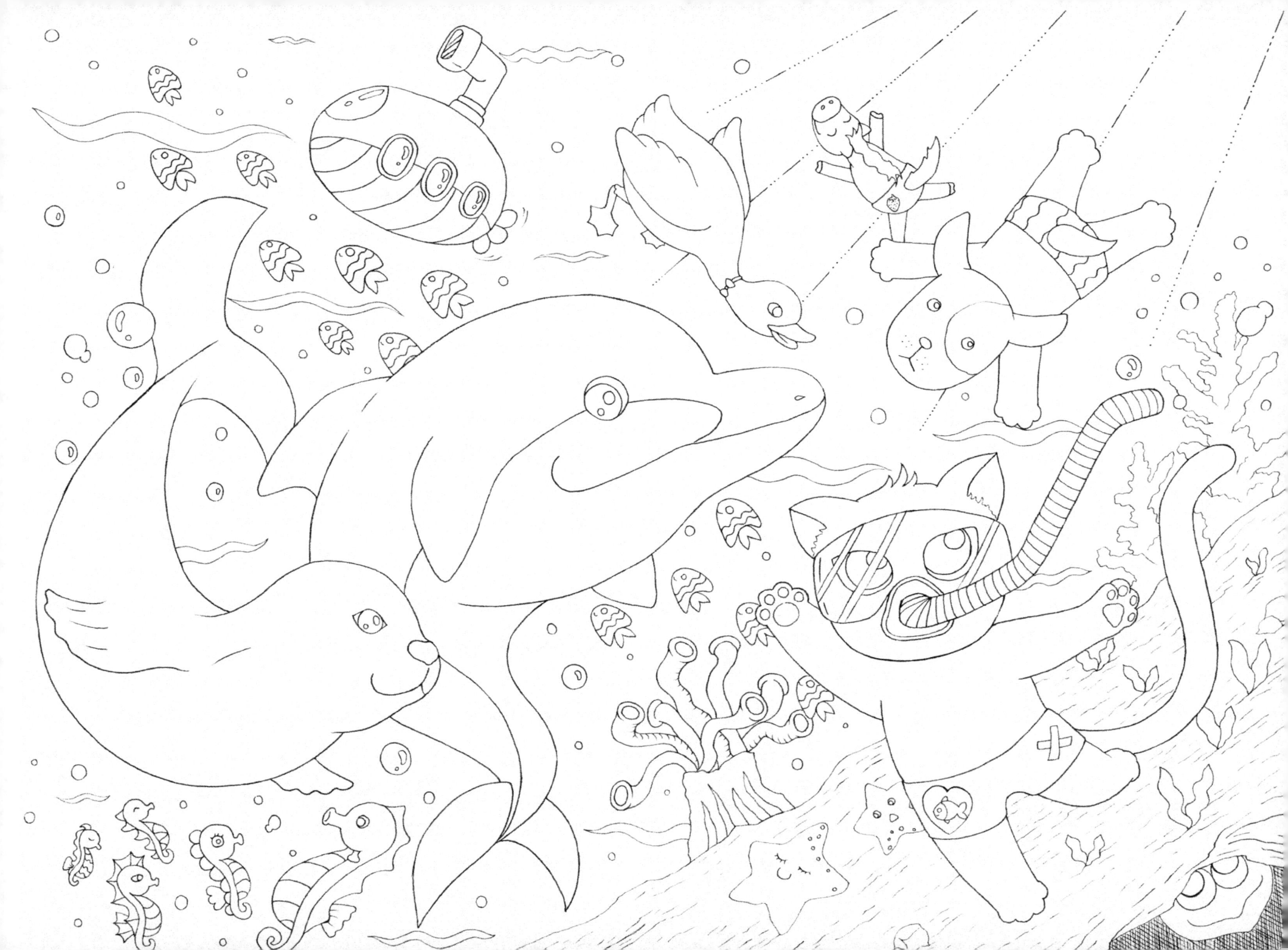

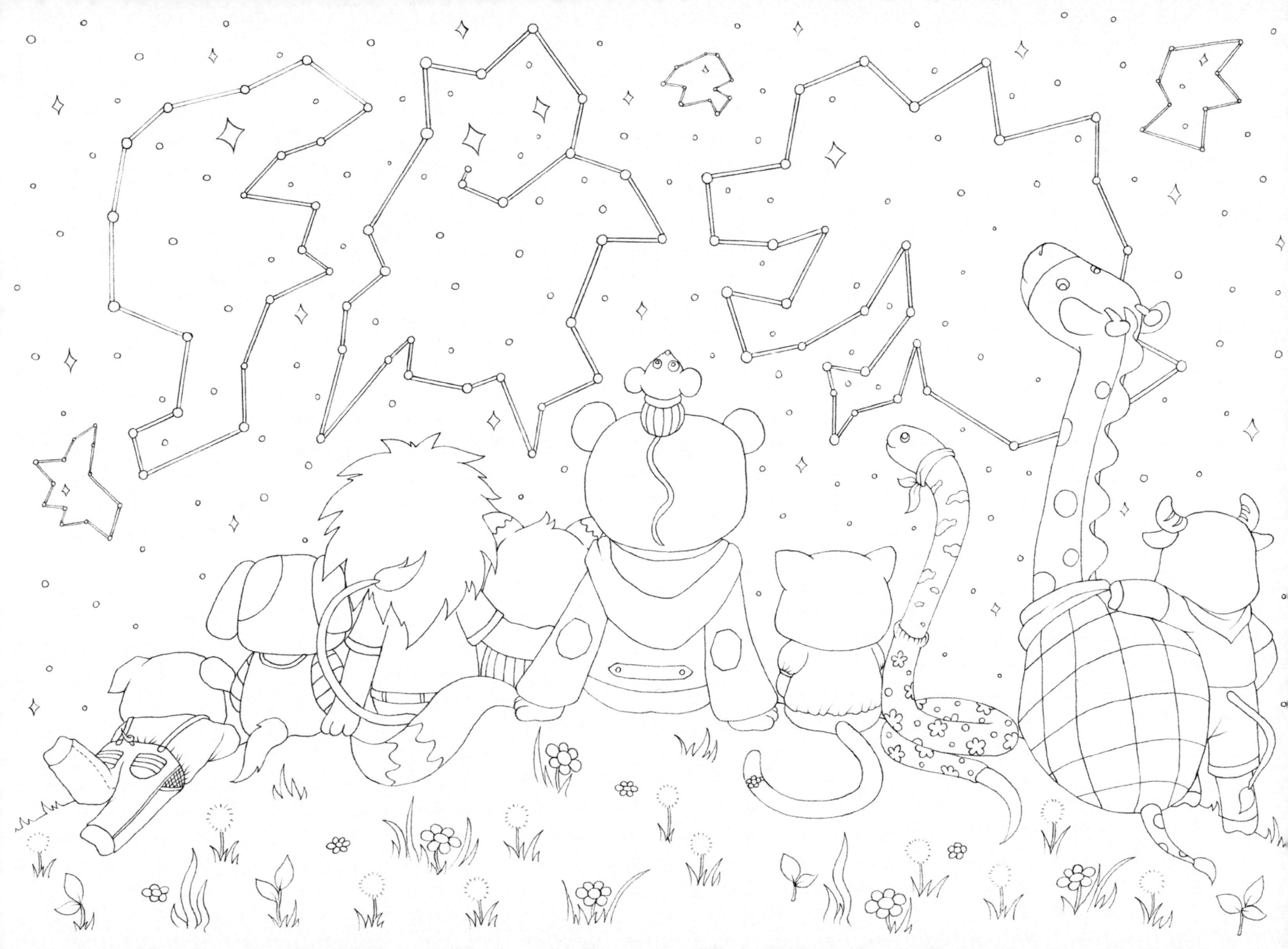